MICHIGAN

To – Ginny & Doug,
my friends!
Thanks
Teri ☺

Symmetry of color along
stone-laden shore of Lake
Superior, near Munising
in Pictured Rocks National
Lakeshore.

MICHIGAN

BY STAN OSOLINSKI

International Standard Book Number 0-912856-34-3

Library of Congress Catalog Number 77-072232

Copyright© 1977 by Publisher • Charles H. Belding

Graphic Arts Center Publishing Co.

2000 N.W. Wilson • Portland, Oregon 97209 • 503/224-7777

Designer • Robert Reynolds

Printer • Graphic Arts Center

Bindery • Lincoln & Allen

Printed in the United States of America

Sun filters through Lake Michigan breaker as it explodes upon confrontation with icy shore.

DEDICATION
For my parents, in grateful appreciation for the assistance which made this book a reality.

Beech leaves add a splash of color along woodland trail in Kensington Metropark. Left: Morning sun pierces timber grove in Seney National Wildlife Refuge. Pages 8 and 9 following: Sunlight fully exposes Canada geese on surface of Kent Lake.

Autumn foliage carpets a forest floor. Right: A remote island and the northern shore of Isle Royale National Park are highlighted by sun shimmering on Lake Superior.

LAND OF WATER

Once, at a time buried somewhere in the dim geologic past, a vast ocean sprayed its saline mist here and rampaging volcanoes angrily spewed forth energies entombed inside themselves for eons. The oceans bequeathed an inheritance of untold wealth in the massive salt deposits underlying modern day Detroit while the volcanoes launched on their trajectory scalding rivers of lava that vaporized the primeval forest and then unleashed titanic forces that lifted solid rock from the water's depths.

Once, then once again, and yet once more, over uncounted centuries, prodigious glaciers imperceptibly crept here inch by relentless inch and bulky mastodons soberly trod an unstable environment. The blankets of ice left the imprint of their repeated advances and retreats on the hilly terrain of much of today's Michigan while the great mammoths deposited their mighty footprints along muddy shorelines and relinquished their sturdy bones to the sands of time.

More recently, primitive tribes of Indians skillfully hunted the area and daring Frenchmen explored the territory in competition with the British. The red man's heritage lives on every time we mention the name of a city such as Kalamazoo, Menominee, Ontonagon and dozens more. The variety of adventurous spirits from explorers and missionaries to trappers and soldiers who sought everything from the pelts of beaver to the souls of Indians handed down a legacy of historical lore that yet survives in such divergent aspects of twentieth century life as western movies and antique collecting.

In comparison to the geologic, historic time period spanned above, it was only mere seconds ago that a motherless 16 year-old named Henry Ford walked resolutely from Dearborn to Detroit in search of a job and a brash youngster from the south by the name of Tyrus Raymond Cobb, sport's unforgettable "Georgia Peach," streaked the basepaths of the American League. The results of Ford's seemingly uneventful hike would one day soon culminate in the formation of the Ford Motor Company with its incredibly successful innovation known as the Model T, while Cobb's magic bat and mercurial spikes would over the course of two decades virtually rewrite the entire baseball record book.

Father Jacques Marquette proselytized here, the celebrated Jolliet explored the region and the affluent John Jacob Astor added to his wealth in the fur trade. Thomas Edison was here and so was Ernest Hemingway, George (later General) Custer, Charles Lindbergh, Robert Frost and so many more.

But long before the advent of the white man upon the scene, Michigan was inhabited by groups of red men who lived in harmony with nature that we today can only hope to imitate. For perhaps as much as 10,000 years before the white man, these bands of semi-nomadic tribesmen hunted and fished and trapped a revered land. Michigan served as both meeting ground and home for three major tribes of Indians. The Chippewas resided mainly in the Upper Peninsula, the Ottawas in the region about the Straits of Mackinac and the Pottawatomis in the southern section of the Lower Peninsula.

Our debt to these Indians probably will never be adequately appreciated or accurately measured, but we in Michigan today owe much to their life-style of yesterday. The villages in which they settled eventually burgeoned into our cities. Detroit, of course, heads the list. Grand Rapids, Pontiac, Kalamazoo, Saginaw, Marquette and an assortment of others were once Indian settlements. Routes taken by Indian trails have now broadened into four-lane highways linking Michigan's major urban areas. The Indians' knowledge of natural ways helped encourage the development of the fur trade in the territory and their introduction of maize to the white man's world had far-reaching implications to this day.

Surely less practical, but perhaps more aesthetic, are the vivid, multi-syllable words that the Indians handed down as names for cities, towns or noticeable features. These names translate into colorful descriptions of a locale's distinctive character: Leelanau, land of delight; Kalamazoo, place where water boils; Michilimackinac (understandably shortened through the ages to Mackinac), the great turtle; Menominee, wild rice country; Munising, place of the island; and others too numerous to list. More than half our counties bear Indian names . . . names of yore that conjure up greater days for the red man . . . names such as Pontiac, Tecumseh, Wyandotte.

Today, there are less than 10,000 Indians in Michigan. Signs of their ancestral forerunners are even fewer and farther between. There are the burial mounds on the Grand River west of Grand Rapids, a handful of petroglyphs in Sanilac county and, most abundant, a variety of arrowheads so treasured by schoolboys.

The seventeenth century ushered in an era that presaged an end to the Indian's sovereign position in the territory, an era that heralded the age of the French. During the years 1618-1619 the Frenchman Etienne Brulé visited the region near Sault Sainte Marie, making him the first known European to reach Michigan. By 1621 or 1622 his later travels had carried him up the St. Mary's River and westward into Lake Superior. This exploration symbolically seemed to initiate the period of French occupation, a significant chapter in the history of Michigan which would last until about the year 1760 when British forces, under the notorious Major Robert Rogers, occupied Detroit and a year later controlled posts at Michilimackinac and St. Joseph to the west. French rule did not officially end though until the year 1763 when the Treaty of Paris ceded control to the English.

In the century and a half that had elapsed since the days of Brulé, numerous events had taken place that would alter the future history of the entire area. In 1634 the French explorer Jean Nicolet had set out in search of the fabled Northwest Passage. Instead he discovered Lake Michigan. So confident had he been of success that he had loaded his canoe with a robe of Chinese damask decorated with birds and flowers, truly proper attire befitting an audience with the oriental emperor whose acquaintance he eagerly anticipated. Passing through the Straits of Mackinac, Nicolet arrived at Green Bay and, no doubt much to his chagrin, discovered, not Cathay, but only Indian villages.

In 1668 the Jesuit priest, Fr. Jacques Marquette, on a mission to the Chippewa Indians, had established at the Soo what is today regarded as the oldest white settlement in the state. Then, in 1679, the *Griffin,* first sailing vessel on the upper Great Lakes, under the command of the famous French empire builder La Salle, carried adventuresome traders to Green Bay, Wisconsin. Its unexplained disappearance on the return voyage remains to this day one of the great mysteries held in trust by the silent waters of the Great Lakes. Shortly thereafter, in 1701, other Frenchmen, under the leadership of one Antoine de la Mothe Cadillac, established a town they dubbed with the phrase "d'etroit," the city "of the straits," a name referring to the 27-mile long Detroit River. As the French and British fought for control of this strategic location during the course of the next 100 years, Detroit was the target of several major battles. Unquestionably the seventeenth century belonged to the French. Their extensive, empire-building exploration created a vast, but thinly-held kingdom which stretched from Detroit to Mackinac.

The eighteenth century, though, witnessed Great Britain's unqualified intrusion into America, an area previously the exclusive domain of the French. The duel for worldwide empire between the two battling nations continued to escalate as the bellicose countries engaged in some eight wars from the last decade of the seventeenth century through the first 15 years of the nineteenth. Britain's upper hand in North America was recognized by the Treaty of Paris in 1763 which secured for them all territory east of the Mississippi, including Michigan, where the British flag flew until 1796.

Initially the French had benefitted in the conflict from the support of the native Indian population, with whom they had lived in peace. Even as late as the early 1760s, the Indians of Michigan, still resentful of the British, banded together under the Ottawa Chieftain Pontiac and terrorized the English in their newly-won city of Detroit. But Pontiac's Rebellion, though the longest Indian military operation of its kind in American history, was short lived, and eventually the British so totally overwhelmed the Indians that they conditionally favored Great Britain during the American Revolution.

After the American Revolution, despite another Treaty of Paris in 1783 which acknowledged the independence of the United States, the British did not evacuate the territory until 1796 when, in June of that year, General Anthony Wayne dispatched one regiment of the army under his command to march into Detroit and receive the surrender of the English. A month later, on July 11, 1796, the star-spangled banner of America was raised to fly for the first time in the breezes above Detroit. But this memorable event was of short duration.

During the War of 1812, when Indians again fought on the British side, Detroit was recaptured and held by the English for most of the war. Not until the summer of 1813 did the tide of battle turn in the Americans' favor. Then, at Put-in-Bay of Lake Erie, the 28-year-old Captain Oliver Hazard Perry led a renovated American navy to victory over the British. This, the decisive battle of the war, also ranks as one of the most important in our history. By the time fighting ended in 1814, the British were gone, the Indians had been driven further west, and the door was opened for rapid expansion.

Settlers came slowly at first; then, with the arrival of the first railroads in the 1830s, more and more swiftly. Under the skillful direction of General Lewis Cass, governor of the Michigan Territory from 1813 to 1831, effective policies were instituted and brought to fruition. Calling upon his earlier experiences as an explorer of the wilderness, Cass detailed to the federal government the possibilities inherent in Michigan's development and prevailed upon them to construct five military highways. By 1818 public land went on sale in Detroit and in 1825 the Erie Canal opened at New York, providing a water access route to Michigan land that was far less strenuous than the traditional overland path. Farmers now arrived on the scene to till the fields and lumbermen constructed sawmills along the rivers to take advantage of the great forests.

In only 20 years the new territory was ready for statehood. Application was made to Congress in 1835, but a boundary dispute with Ohio over the southern border led to the bloodless Toledo War. Much more vocal than vicious, the quarrel resulted in Michigan conceding the disputed strip at its southern edge to Ohio and Indiana in exchange for the western two-thirds of the Upper Peninsula. Congress followed in 1837 by granting admission approval to Michigan as the twenty-sixth state of the Union. Detroit served as the capital of the new state until Lansing replaced it in March of 1847. There the seat of Michigan's government has since resided. The capitol building begun in 1872 and formally opened in 1879, is a dignified structure created of marble quarried in Vermont, tin from Wales and plate glass from England, all enhanced with doorknobs and chandeliers of native copper to symbolize Michigan's natural wealth.

Those years immediately preceding and closely following statehood witnessed rapid changes in Michigan's vocational emphasis. In the beginning, fur trading and trapping had been the main attractions. By 1808, when John Jacob Astor headquartered his American Fur Company at Mackinac Island, the fur trade had grown to be the state's first major industry. Even Michigan's nickname of the "Wolverine State" attests to the importance of trapping. There is no conclusive evidence to prove that these large weasels, accounting for only an infinitesimal fraction of a fur market dominated by beaver skins, ever actually lived in the state. But their pelts, arriving at Sault Sainte Marie's northern relay center for shipment to Great Lakes and Mississippi markets, somehow came to be associated with the state as their point of origin and the name persisted. The English developed the fur trade beyond the levels attained by the French, but the rapacious assault upon Michigan's fur-bearing mammals could not continue unabated and by 1840 many trappers had moved westward.

There is little doubt that the decline was even further accelerated by the 1844 discovery of iron ore in the Upper Peninsula near present-day Negaunee. Lured by this prospect of a new and greater wealth, many workers gave up their previous trade to endure a taxing and often hazardous occupation involving themselves in some aspect of the growing mining industry.

The early miners themselves faced what was by far the most exceedingly dangerous situation. As surface supplies were depleted within the first three decades, mine shafts bit into the earth's entrails by the 1870s. Here, miners hoped that the pitiful candles which lit their way would not extinguish themselves in a sudden draft and cast them into a pall of darkness; they further trusted that the wooden support beams would not weaken, collapse and entomb them beneath a pile of rubble. For many, the harsh reality of the work dimmed the romanticized dream of sudden riches that they had envisioned. In the dust of their despair remained emptied shafts and abandoned town sites.

Almost simultaneous to the discovery of iron ore was the unearthing of copper. Though some of the prehistoric Indians had known of its presence, they had utilized only the visible veins to fashion their desired tools. The first white man to knowingly glimpse the valued mineral was the Jesuit priest Fr. Claude Allouez, who as early as 1666 had described its presence along the south shore of Lake Superior. Nearly 200 years passed, however, before an 1843 treaty between the United States government and the Chippewa Indians opened the district around today's Copper Harbor to mining. Soon Michigan's mining of copper led the nation, a position that was maintained well into the 1880s. The combined lodes at Calumet produced the incredible total of over 4 billion pounds of copper during peak operative years. Even today Michigan ranks a fluctuating fifth or sixth in the production of copper and second in iron as lower grade deposits continue to be extracted from that mineral-laden portion of the western Upper Peninsula that has long been called "Copper Country."

Although copper and iron attracted most of the early attention by the turn of the century gypsum, limestone and salt assumed a place of importance in the mining development of Michigan. In today's world, gypsum, wrested from the central portions of the state, is deployed essentially for the production of plasterboard. Limestone, excavated from the world's largest open limestone quarry at Rogers City along Lake Huron, is then directly loaded onto freighters waiting to disperse it across the world for a variety of purposes. Salt, whose mining is now centered around Midland, where the crystals are accumulated by the evaporation of natural or artifical brines, and at Detroit, where rock salt is scooped out by the deep-shaft method, predominantly provides, not our common table salt, but rather the raw material which forms the basis of the state's remarkable chemical and pharmaceutical industries.

Accompanying the growth of the mining industry was a booming logging business. White pine, now the state tree, was then the wood most sought after for use in construction, and abounded in the woodlands of northern Michigan. By 1869, less than 40 years after admission to the Union, Michigan was the leading lumber-producing state in the nation. The muscular arms and brawny backs of immigrant lumberjacks supplied the strength which supported this position of leadership for some 30 years, far into the 1890s when the lumbering boom crested its economic peak. But as the lumbermen harvested the virgin forests, they left behind for twentieth century conservationists a scarred timberland sorely in need of reforestation. The great forests that had made Grand Rapids the furniture capital of the nation and had rebuilt Chicago after the Great Fire of 1871 have long since been leveled. Other forests, which in the final decades of the nineteenth century had carried Menominee, meaning "wild rice", to the position of the largest pine shipping port in the world, have been exhausted.

Following the disappearance of the lumberjack and the logger came a rash of fires. Fed by the cuttings left behind by the work gangs, the conflagrations were ignited in late summer as the cut-over land became bone dry. The most terrible fire in Michigan's history raged through the thumb area in September of 1881.

Over 1,000,000 acres of farmland were destroyed and more than 100 people died. The disaster did, however, spark one unexpected benefit. The newly-founded American Red Cross provided aid for the distraught victims who thereby garnered the initial relief furnished by this now world-famous ever alert humanitarian organization.

With the decline of logging, agriculture soon stepped to the forefront on the cleared lands as the new farmers took full advantage of the fertile soils in the south and the prime weather conditions along Lake Michigan in the west.

In retrospect, one can see in each of these successive stages a decided pattern emerging for Michigan in the final years of the 1800's and the first years of the 1900's. Michigan's structure was becoming less and less natural. The sun, while setting on the day of the trapper, fur trader, miner and lumberman was rising on the era of the factory worker, white collar man and scientist.

The depletion of the natural wealth that had attracted earlier settlers and the discovery of greater wealth in new explorations beyond the state helped to bring down the final curtain on this phase of Michigan's growth. Westward expansion had now opened to farmland the immense sweep of the plains and prairies of mid-America. Discovery of iron ore in the Mesabi Range in Minnesota promised a treasure that would dwarf Michigan's supply of that metal. Copper had burst onto the scene in Montana, Arizona and other western states. The new generation migrated west with each individual seeking his own personal fortune of gold at the end of a mineral rainbow.

No longer was Michigan on the outskirts of American civilization. It was now a well-developed, well-populated state. By 1910, the change in succession from a trapping, mining, logging and farming society to a manufacturing center had been completed. After 1910, more than half the population was residing in urban rather than rural areas.

In 1908, for better or worse, Henry Ford introduced to the world his Model T. In that same year, William C. Durant merged Buick, Cadillac and Oldsmobile to create General Motors. Although the idea of the "horseless carriage" had been toyed with and even embodied since the 1880s, Detroit, with its automobile factories, now quickly more than doubled its population and became an international symbol of America's productive strength.

Today, as unchallenged automobile capital of the world, Detroit and subsidiaries based in other Michigan cities are responsible for a major share of all car and truck production in the United States. The Ford Rouge Plant in Dearborn is the largest industrial complex in the world. Economists still look to Detroit, an exciting dynamic metropolis, as a barometer of the nation's financial health. But the city offers both residents and visitors much more than its automotive production, a fact foreseen by the seventeenth century Recollect priest, Father Louis Hennepin, who penned the following sentence of the then new French settlement: "Those who will one day have the happiness to possess this fertile and pleasant strait will be much obliged to those who have shown them the way."

Today, in spite of the sometimes serious social problems of a large metropolitan network, there is still happiness for twentieth century Detroiters who live along that "pleasant strait" now known as the Detroit River. This, the very route which ferried Cadillac ashore more than 200 years ago, is today one of the busiest water routes on earth. It is also the site of the Ambassador Bridge which reaches across the river in a symbolic handshake of steel to clasp the shore of Michigan's neighbors in Windsor, Ontario, thereby uniting Canadians and Americans in an international gesture of friendship and peace. Below the busy waters, the Detroit-Windsor Tunnel imports and exports daily visitors and workers between the two friendly nations.

Just east of the downtown area, the river harbors Belle Isle, a thousand-acre island park that is home to the Children's Zoo, the oldest still-operative aquarium in America, and a conservatory of many plants. Native squirrels, deer from the Orient and migratory waterfowl reside here to delight thousands of harried city dwellers who look to the natural beauties which yet remain as they boat, fish, jog or simply observe the island's treasures.

The Huron-Clinton Metropolitan Authority administers ten Metroparks that offer beaches, forests, golf courses, nature centers and much more in a five-county system surrounding Detroit.

World-famous Greenfield Village and Henry Ford Museum in Dearborn re-create America as it was in the nineteenth century for thousands and thousands of tourists each year. The Detroit Zoological Park has earned national recognition for its freedom of movement exhibit areas and for the work it has done on breeding endangered species in captivity. The Institute of Arts, the Historical Museum and the Main Public Library host cultural events throughout the year.

Here are hundreds of urban, industrial plants where coal and iron, aluminum and rubber are fused and transformed into the necessary automobiles and trucks and tractors. But here also are quiet woods and fields, where other plants, far different in nature, combine sun and air, soil and water to produce needed sugars and cellulose and oxygen for anxious consumers.

On the blackened pavement of Metropolitan Airport a silver-winged jet taxies down the runway. Nearby, a handful of male mallards with glistening green heads splash into a sun-dappled pond. In the concrete-covered city, 10,000 housewives crowd neighborhood supermarkets in search of foodstuffs to stock the family cupboards. Elsewhere, at the edge of a grass-covered meadow, a vixen fox patrols her territory in search of mice for her recently-weaned young. Less noticed, but no less attractive in its own way, is the splashing array of colors and scents employed by spring wildflowers along a woodland brook to woo their insect pollinators.

It may surprise the reader to discover that these urban and natural worlds still exist together within a few dozen miles of Detroit. Exploring the interface of man and nature in and around the Motor City, I believe we need an increased awareness in our society of what we stand to lose in terms of the potential disappearance of wild animals and native plants.

The "concrete" benefits of nature should be obvious to us all. Towering skyscrapers lift their heads to the heavens only after they have literally risen from the mineral bowels of the earth. Esoteric volumes which line our library shelves were once the trees that graced a pristine forest. But how does one measure the "intangible" values of nature? What is the value sprightly chipmunks provide campers, hikers and photographers? Who can place a price tag on the value of clean water for boaters, fishermen and swimmers?

As we shoot forth our branches into new and exciting technological realms, we should not forget the natural roots from which we all have sprung.

I'll always remember the horned lark that nested one March on the playground of the school where I once taught. She must have surveyed and triangulated that area very carefully for she had homesteaded in a site so precisely located as to involve herself in nearly every one of our scheduled athletic activities. Two seventh-grade boys had excitedly furnished me with the information on its whereabouts.

"Mr. O, Mr. O, there's a bird nest out back."

I immediately posted a small wooden sign: "Maternity Ward —Please Do Not Disturb." That afternoon I informed all the classes of its presence and value.

Arriving very early at school the next morning, I spied the expectant mother nattily perched on my crude artwork. Before I could ready my 500 mm lens, she flitted away, and I never again saw her on that stake. However, that single missed photograph could never have equalled the many other benefits the little bird provided our students. For 17 days, nearly 600 youngsters carefully avoided disturbing the well-camouflaged nest and counseled the unaware when they approached it too closely.

Third base ended up in some weird places that spring, and I know of one end zone on a certain football field that was never scored upon in post-school pick-up games. But the horned lark didn't miss her "field" goal; she successfully hatched both of the eggs she had laid. On lunch hour the younger grades would line up behind my 640 mm telephoto lens to peek in on the progress our adopted family was making. Eventually one young bird was to die a natural death, while the other apparently flew off one day to take its place in that part of the world around Detroit still suitable for horned larks.

That same schoolyard provided a convenient backdrop for many other natural experiences for my students. I am confident that many of those happenings will be long remembered by those now mature children that I will never see again. I can even wistfully imagine that a handful of them may at this very moment be perusing these contents and mentally traveling backwards in time to those days of discovery.

In spring there were killdeer every morning in that field; in fall, flocks of herring gulls up from the Detroit River to feed upon the bugs stirred up from the short grasses by football cleats. There was the one-eyed bullfrog that sunned himself along the footpath that paralleled the drain creek at the field's south end. Muskrats and turtles captured in that creek and brought into class produced their share of havoc in upsetting the school routine, but they also led to some spontaneously profitable learning experiences for the children about animals and their human counterparts.

One day at afternoon recess, when crystalline sun dogs were ringing a pale April sun, a sharp-eyed third-grader spotted a tiny speck hovering above the parking lot—a red-tailed hawk. From that day forward we looked for him each afternoon, and we saw him on more than a few occasions. Pine warblers, cottontails, garter snakes, ovenbirds and a score of other wild animals would take their turns in the spotlight over the course of some nine years. But to me, the wonder of it all is that everything happened only a few minutes away from one of the major interchanges of Interstate Highway 94, which passes the school less than one mile to the south.

Beyond the nine-to-three world of the school, I also encountered many other unforgettable moments of nature that were among the city, but not of the city. I recall the Canada goose who nested on a small point of land jutting into a lake that was located across the street from a public golf course. The first week of photographing the bird and her vigilant mate revealed five eggs when the female rose off the nest. The second week showed that one of the eggs had been replaced by a golf ball, substituted no doubt by some frustrated duffer.

Other moments that come to mind would have to include applying the brakes and swerving the high performance car out of the way of a red fox who raced from nowhere across the Lodge Expressway as I drove to photograph the sunrise; summer baseball practice being enriched by the nightly appearance of purple martins and nighthawks swooping above the diamond, no doubt catching "flies" of their own along with other seasonally abundant insects of dusk; the snowy owl, tenant of north polar regions, perched on department store window ledges along Woodward Avenue, the main artery of downtown Detroit; the kestrels, or sparrow hawks, who nested in the billboard steps away from Cobo Hall's impressive convention center.

The stories are many, but I trust the point is well-taken. Nature does not die easily. Plants, animals and landscapes that have evolved over thousands of centuries possess a tenacity which their often delicate appearance would seem to belie.

The spacious fields where I once slugged out resounding batting averages a dozen summers ago (or is it two dozen already?) now lie cemented under six lanes of the car-choked Southfield Expressway. But I still see a red-tailed hawk gripping a limb on one of the trees planted along the embankment directly across from Ford's World Headquarters. Best of all, though, is the fact that *real* pheasants with *real* feathers still burst from the grasses and fly directly over the roofs of speeding steel machines with names like Cougar and Roadrunner, Rabbit and Impala!

The great hardwood forest essentially disappeared from this part of the planet long ago, but opossums, raccoons and an occasional skunk still make a nuisance of themselves in the refuse cans and garages of accountants, lawyers and computer programmers less than ten miles from Kennedy Square in the heart of the downtown area.

With their insensitive faces of brick the uniform homes of suburbia stare remorsefully at a brave new world. Yet I still catch an infrequent glimpse of a flaming scarlet tanager in the sparse woods remaining. Cardinals, catbirds and song sparrows are regular patrons of the birdfeeder in the backyard of my parent's suburban Livonia home. I recently blinked my eyes in wonder as I looked out the front window and watched a half-dozen bobwhites parade over the front lawn, across the sidewalk, past the neighbor's garage and then into the shrubbery adjoining their residence.

Ribbons of concrete highways invade and interrupt much of the unspoiled habitat sorely needed by dwindling wildlife populations, but they also safely convey nature buffs to nearby sanctuaries such as Kensington Metropark. Here, less than 30 miles from the din of the city and its nearly 4 million metropolitan inhabitants, you can look for birds as rare as a sandhill crane or a turkey vulture, an osprey or even a rare bald eagle.

Surprisingly, the peace and beauty of the natural world is still to be found close to our largest city. I can only hope that we shall have the foresight to conserve it.

But Detroit is not Michigan's only city nor its only region with a claim to fame. The town of Holland, settled by the Dutch in 1847, has merited the title "Tulip Capital of America." The city of almost 30,000 people annually celebrates its position of pre-eminence with the famed Tulip Festival that for one week in May balloons its population to a quarter million sightseers who come from across the country to witness the spectacular display of myriad tulips in bloom.

The northern village of Interlochen hosts the National Music Camp, the largest outdoor music training center in the world. At Indian River stands the world's largest bronze and wood crucifix. The cross, made of one California redwood tree, stands 55 feet high and supports a seven ton statue sculptured by Marshall Fredericks, living in Birmingham, also responsible for the Spirit of Detroit figure at the base of Woodward Avenue.

Jackson merits note as the place where, on July 6, 1854, in a small oak grove, a group of about 1,500 discontented Whigs put the finishing touches on the founding and creating of the Republican Party. At East Lansing is Michigan State University, the first land grant college in America. Established in 1855 as an agricultural college, it has since expanded into one of the nation's largest universities.

Ishpeming in the Upper Peninsula is home of the National Ski Hall of Fame. At Grand Haven, on Lake Michigan, spouts the world's largest musical fountain, designed with a versatility that is capable of producing the mind-boggling total of two QUADRILLION variations of color and form through an incredible network of wires and pipes.

Finally there is Mackinac Island, recently designated the most historical site in Michigan. Old Fort Mackinac, overlooking the strategic harbor since 1780, has been restored and preserved as a living museum. Within walking distance stands the imposing Grand Hotel. Erected in 1887, it is the largest summer hotel in the world. Also boasting the longest colonial porch anywhere, it is one of the great man-made landmarks of the Great Lakes.

So it has happened that the larger-than-life legends of Michigan's geologic and historic yesterdays are today replaced by a new breed of giants far different in stature.

For here now is General Motors, the industrial giant that spurs the very heart of the American economy. Here is Kellogg's, the world's largest producer of ready-made cereals that has altered the breakfast eating habits of an entire nation. Here, too, courses mighty Superior, greatest of the Great Lakes and the largest supply of fresh water in the world. Here are the Soo Locks, the largest and busiest navigational route of their kind in the world, handling more cargo than the Panama and Suez Canals combined. Here is the University of Michigan, one of the nation's most outstanding institutions of higher learning that also maintains the largest college stadium in America and at Peach

Mountain operates a radio telescope capable of probing the interstellar depths of space for waves nearly a half billion years old. Here, in Oceana county, prospers the largest cherry orchard in the world, where nature's bounty and man's ingenuity combine to produce and process an almost unbelievable 600 tons of fruit a day in season.

In this state of superlatives, the contrasts of past and present are striking. Where giant-sized reptilian quadrupeds may once have battled for supremacy of the earth, diminutive Kirtland warblers, one of America's rarest birds, now struggle for their very existence. Where prehistoric seas once tossed their waters against a long vanished shore, row upon row of apple blossoms emit refreshing aromas as they waft in the gentle breezes of Lake Michigan. But one need not look only to the past for the contrasts of Michigan. They are also here today for the observant visitor or resident to notice and enjoy.

From the flat farmland along the eastern thumb of Lake Huron to the more than 100 waterfalls of the Upper Peninsula; from the remnant forests of white pine to the rugged majesty of Superior's surf-battered Pictured Rocks National Lakeshore; from some 11,000 inland lakes to the ever-changing panorama of shifting sand dunes; from boundless meadows of delicate wildflowers in the southwest to over 200 inches of annual snowfall in numerous northern communities, Michigan truly offers living proof of the motto which appears on the state seal: "Si quaeris peninsulam amoenam, circumspice"—If you seek a pleasant peninsula, look about you.

By all means look. Look at the golden waters of irrepressible Tahquamenon as they plunge 48 feet over sandstone cliffs before flowing onward to the cascading Lower Falls. Look at the incredible riot of fall color that paints the countryside in autumn. Look at the occasional bald eagle that still successfully nests in spite of shrinking habitat and the presence of now banned, but yet persistent pesticides.

But do more than look about. See not only with the physical eye, but also with the eye of the mind and the heart. The woodland trail which may be looked at in less than an hour may never be really seen at all until you've spent a day, a month or even a season along it. The robin that you glimpse on the way to work all spring and summer may not be understood until you have watched him search out a worm, build a nest or start a migration that will carry him a third of a continent away. Lastly, the gently curving river that you have been viewing from your cottage window for some 20 years may never be appreciated until you see its once forested shores uprooted and supplanted by an industrial complex spewing noxious effluents into the previously untroubled waters.

No narrative of present-day Michigan is complete without mentioning its waters. Even the name of the state derives from a variety of Indian syllables such as Mischiganong or Mishi Gamaw which loosely translate into Great Water or the Great Lake in reference to Lake Michigan. Automobile license plates once proudly proclaimed Michigan as the "Great Lake State," with an excess of 11,000 inland lakes plus all but one of the five Great Lakes bathing its shores.

The significance of water in the natural and human history of the state cannot possibly be exaggerated or overstated. The powerful influence of the waters in and around Michigan either directly or indirectly exerts itself on everything from fishing to farming, tourism to transportation and a great deal in-between. Together with their adjoining river systems, the Great Lakes represent the largest supply of fresh water in the world. With 95,000 square miles of area, Superior, Huron, Michigan, Erie and Ontario provide an invaluable natural resource which amply cares for not only the natural creatures who have been resident since time immemorial but also for the mankind who now seeks his reward from the bountiful waters. The Great Lakes also rank as the world's greatest inland waterway, giving Michigan water access to seven states, Ontario, Canada and, via the St. Lawrence Seaway, the entire world.

The very presence of the Great Lakes bestows upon Michigan

much of its industrial, agricultural and recreational character. From the earliest days when the canoes of the Indians and the French fur traders slipped silently along their shores, these watery highways have played a major role in the development and civilization of Michigan. In the days of yore the birch barks may have ferried nothing larger than a few pelts, sacks of food or necessary supplies and tools. Today, massive freighters, carrying more than 100 million tons of grain, ores and manufactured goods to a waiting world, ply these very waters with frames so drastically elongated from bow to stern that they exceed the combined length of two football fields.

The Great Lakes determine much of our climate and, in the process are responsible for a substantial portion of our highly prosperous agriculture. Michigan's weather, dominated by the meteorology of the Lakes, produces expectedly brusque and blustery days on more than a few occasions each year. From spring through autumn, rain falls nearly one day in every three; by winter there are extended periods of cloudiness in most zones. However, the geographic mitten that lower Michigan resembles most often snuggles with acceptable comfort between the protective waters that shield the Lower Peninsula on east and west. Mollified by these waters, summer and winter winds moderate Michigan's seasons, generating a climate devoid of the harsh extremes to be found in any other state of equal northern latitude, yet at the same time fashioning a welcome variety of seasonal changes.

The winds' tempering of the weather in turn creates an agriculture of vast proportions, especially along the sandy coasts of Lake Michigan, where apples and peaches are harvested in abundance and where one-third of the entire world production of red tart cherries is processed. The area of Traverse City, locale of the National Cherry Festival, by itself prepares 50 million pounds of cherries for world markets each year. This fortuitous combination of mild weather, fertile soil and a relatively long growing season makes Michigan probably the most self-sufficient food producing state in our nation.

During the nineteenth century the teeming waters of the Great Lakes gave birth to a thriving commercial fishing industry and, with improved transportation in each succeeding decade of the twentieth century, a booming tourist trade took full advantage of the recreational opportunities afforded by the waters, the beaches and their accompanying scenery.

Although the fishing business flourished on enormous catches of whitefish and lake trout in the late 1800s and even well into the 1900s, it would steadily lessen in importance, a fact attested to by the appearance of more and more abandoned fishing villages. Many Great Lake and inland waters still swarm with a plentiful supply of fish to lure some commercial fishermen and weekend anglers. Trout, salmon, perch, bass, sturgeon, walleye and muskellunge all claim a following of ardent supporters who prize their scaly catch as the tastiest or gamiest.

The demise of a prolific commercial fishing industry did not victimize the state as sorely as one might imagine for soon to rise in its ashes was a new wave of prosperity. Vacationers arrived from across the country in ever increasing numbers not only to fish, but also to boat and water ski by summer, then snow ski, snowmobile and ice skate through winter. Today, boaters with craft ranging from the oar-propelled canoes paddled by vacationing Sunday school teachers on placid northern lakes to the unlimited hydroplanes of the Gold Cup races pushed to their mechanical limits by professional drivers powering along the foaming Detroit River at speeds well in excess of 100 miles per hour all enjoy the watery realm at their own level. This year-round, water-oriented recreation moved tourism into third place as a revenue producer for the state, trailing only manufacturing and agriculture. Then in 1976, for the first time, the 10 million plus tourists who spend part or all of their vacation here in the Water Wonderland kindled the financial energy for it to leapfrog agriculture into the runner-up position.

The waters of the Great Lakes further conferred upon Michigan the almost totally overlooked distinction of having the longest state coastline until Alaska was admitted to statehood in 1959. Contrary to popular belief, until that year, this honor did not belong to the better publicized states of Florida or California. In fact, Michigan's 3,000 plus miles of shoreline give it more coast than Florida and California *combined*. A second fact of little note is that when one combines the water area over which Michigan has jurisdiction to its land mass, the state rates as the biggest east of the Mississippi. Encompassing about 96,000 square miles, Michigan is actually larger than the entire country of England. Finally, no resident in the state is more than 85 miles from one of the Great Lakes and no place is more than 15 minutes from some lake or river.

As mentioned earlier, even the name of our state derives from the water discovered here. Algonquian Indian tribes used the term MISCHIGANONG, meaning the Great Lake, to refer to present day Lake Michigan. Although it may have been the *great* lake, the *greatest* lay yet further to the north. The French called it *superieur* merely to indicate that its geographic location placed it *above* Lake Huron. Today we know that, so far as pure size is concerned, Lake Superior outstrips all other fresh water lakes in the world. Some 350 miles long, 160 miles across at its maximum width and reaching more than 1,000 feet deep at its greatest depths, the mighty "Gitche Gumee" of Longfellow occupies some 31,000 square miles of the planet, investing it with real estate enough to make islands of the states of Vermont, New Hampshire, New Jersey, Delaware and Rhode Island, with over 1,000 square miles of open water left.

This sheer size and significance of the Great Lakes frequently overshadows the other watery features here, especially the engrossing variety of beautiful waterfalls in the Upper Peninsula. Although Laughing Whitefish is the tallest of the more than 100 falls and rapids, the surging Tahquamenon is considered by the majority of people to be the most spectacular. The Upper Falls, 200 feet wide with a plunge of nearly 50 feet, is second in size only to Niagara east of the Mississippi.

Rivers such as the Grand, Muskegon and Kalamazoo travel tortuous, twisting routes across the Lower Peninsula as they seek their natural outlet into Lake Michigan. Swamps, marshes and trembling bogs harbor insectivorous vegetation such as the sundew and pitcher plant along with Michigan's only poisonous snake, the seldom seen Massasauga rattlesnake. Mineral springs at Mount Clemens, though reeking with the odor of sulphur, were endured by many for their reputed powers to heal an assortment of woes. Though the business is now defunct, spa operators for a time developed the region into a well-known health resort as they pumped the mineral-laden waters from a depth of over 2,000 feet.

But intermittently in the course of human history man has looked upon the forms of nature's waterworks here not as divine blessings but as formidable obstacles. In at least two such locations, the Straits of Mackinac and the St. Mary's River Falls at Sault Sainte Marie, human endeavors of titanic proportions have resulted in a pair of man's finest engineering achievements, represented by the Mackinac Bridge, connector of the two disparate peninsulas across nearly five miles of water, and the Soo Locks, unequalled for their navigational significance.

Of the 48 contiguous states Michigan is unique in being comprised of two distinct land masses, the Upper and Lower Peninsulas, which are separated from each other by the Straits of Mackinac. Before the completion of "Big Mac," crossing was limited to a time consuming, inefficient ferry trip. But finally, after almost a century of dreaming and nearly four years of arduous construction time, at a cost of nearly $100 million, the steel link was completed and officially opened on November 1, 1957. When measured between its anchorage blocks, an immense span of 8,614 feet, the Mackinac Bridge ranks as the greatest overall suspension bridge in the world even though the Verrazano-Narrows Bridge in New York and the Golden Gate Bridge in San Francisco both possess longer suspension spans. In 1959, the American Institute of Steel Construction awarded "Mighty Mac" the title of "America's Most Beautiful Bridge."

Less than 60 miles to the north of the great bridge, at the Canadian-American border, stretch the Soo Locks, longest and busiest in the world. Here natural forces again taxed man's inventive power to solve a vexing problem. This time, upon the site where Lake Superior connects with Lake Huron via the St. Mary's River Falls, it was approximately a 22-foot drop in the water level from Superior to Huron. The resultant rapids prevented passage of large boats until 1855 when the finished construction allowed the first ships to pass through the locks. Improved and enlarged over the years, the Soo Locks now surpass in seven months the annual traffic and tonnage of both the Panama and Suez Canals combined. With the opening of the beneficial St. Lawrence Seaway in 1959, these locks brought Detroit closer to European ports than New York.

But far more than its waters made Michigan such a desirable parcel of land first for the Indians and later for explorers, trappers and pioneers. The state was, and still is, rich in many other natural features, including its wildlife, minerals, soils and remnant stretches of pine and hardwood forests which once shaded nearly the entire state.

To insure their preservation, local, state and federal agencies have established in Michigan four National Forests and numerous State Forests which together conserve an area of more than 12 million acres. Some of these sanctuaries afford total protection for all trees, from alders and aspens to walnuts and willows. Others permit logging, but now require reforestation, a scientific method which replants for tomorrow the crop that has been harvested for today. Under this protective aegis of up-to-date conservation practices, the second-growth woodlands of modern Michigan, both natural and managed, still account for endless hours of industrial and recreational use.

Finding haven within these refuges is the varied wildlife supported by such an ecosystem. Fluctuating herds of whitetail deer annually number more than a half million animals, making them the most abundant big game mammal in the state. But also right at home in Michigan's woods is an assortment of smaller mammals. Masked raccoons, whose nocturnal forays carry even to the edges of suburbia, den in lofty forest apartments by day. Red and gray squirrels range over a variety of forest conditions, the fox squirrel spending life more adaptable to the urban area. Personable chipmunks stuff mouth pouches with as many seeds as they can hold while they scurry about their daily routine. Cottontail rabbits and snowshoe hares browse the edges and retreat to ground-level brambles or subterranean burrows when danger threatens. Less commonly seen, the striped skunk and the marsupial opossum are omnivorous feeders who do little that warrants their maligned reputation.

Further to the north, black bears feed on the fall harvest of berries as they fatten themselves on every food in sight before retiring to a seasonal state of semi-hibernation which will see the female give birth to what is normally a set of twin cubs sometime in mid-winter. Porcupines use the large incisor teeth characteristic of rodents to strip the bark from treetop cafeterias. The water-dwelling beaver, though not strictly a denizen of the woods, frequents the forest for his sustenance too. This furry lumberjack of the north country, whose valued pelts fashioned the early fur trading and trapping industry, tirelessly chisels down tree after tree that he utilizes not only to construct his renowned dam, but also to build his lodge and to store as an underwater, refrigerated food supply by winter.

There are also woodchucks, red foxes, weasels and others who make a living along the transition zone from forest to field or stream. But a touch of irony has decreed that the most publicized occupant of Michigan forests shall not be a mammal at all. Rather it is a miniscule songbird known as Kirtland's warbler. Birdwatchers from Maine to Oregon migrate yearly to Michigan in the hopes of catching sight of this rare, five-inch long songster who is currently on the endangered species list. A highly selective home builder, the Kirtland's warbler nests only in Michigan and then only in forests of selected jack pines of the proper heighth in a few counties.

In recent years biologists have undertaken a program of deliberate, but controlled, forest fire burns to create nesting conditions suitable for this exceptional feathered friend. The brown-headed cowbirds who parasitize the warbler's nest represent a second major threat, but they are currently being trapped in mist nets and then removed. With only 400 or so nesting in the entire world, Kirtland's warblers need all the help we can give them, so even well-intentioned nature lovers and eager photographers are diverted from the birds' nesting sites during the critical spring period.

The United States Department of the Interior has also designated that a number of the other salient features that comprise a priceless part of Michigan's natural heritage are worthy of protection on a federal level. These areas encompass Pictured Rocks and Sleeping Bear Dunes National Lakeshores; Seney, Shiawassee and Wyandotte National Wildlife Refuges; and one gem of a National Park, Isle Royale in the northwest corner of Lake Superior, where all travel is on foot or by boat.

Isle Royale itself, largest island in a wilderness archipelago consisting of more than 200 smaller islets, spans 45 miles of Superior's sparkling, white-capped waters. In many respects this wild land remains essentially as it was when first described by the Frenchman Brulé and later seventeenth century explorers. Its primitive forests of spruce and fir, birch and aspen still host nearly 30 varieties of wild orchids, more than 200 species of birds and a number of other animals who were able to either fly, swim or drift across the 15 miles or more of water that separate the islands from the nearest mainland. This unique wilderness, accessible only by boat or float-plane, is not penetrated by so much as a single road, but it is pierced by the occasionally-heard howling of the resident pack of timber wolves whose arrival sometime during the winter of 1948-49 was made possible only by the frozen lake which conveyed them on their icy deliverance from the mainland to the islands. Prowling the volcanic rocks in packs of up to a dozen animals, the wolves cull the island's moose population in a cyclic ecological balance that has been the object of many environmental studies on predator/prey relationships.

Not until 1783 did Isle Royale become a part of the United States and even then it was still recognized as Chippewa territory until the year 1843 when the tribe ceded it to the American government. Less than 100 years later, in April of 1940, its dedication as a National Park assured that its special glories would be preserved for all time as a living museum of natural forces.

Perhaps the most unusual and certainly the most captivating story of our two National Lakeshores comes from the romantic tale which records the history involved in both the formation and the naming of the Sleeping Bear Dune. Indian legend tells of a female black bear and her two cubs who were attempting to escape a Wisconsin forest fire by swimming across Lake Michigan. As the tiring cubs faltered behind, Mother Bear crept onto the Michigan shore and lay down to watch the waters for her approaching young. They never made it; and, as the sands covered her waiting body, she became the Sleeping Bear Dune while the two tiny islands offshore represent her vanished cubs.

Within the boundaries of our National Park and our two National Lakeshores wolves, mink, beaver, red fox and birds, all find sanctuary from the advancing onslaught of human hordes. In theory, this protection is granted to great and small alike, without distinction: from the largest, 800-pound bull moose browsing an unpolluted pond of Isle Royale to the tiniest, fraction-of-an-ounce spider resting unobtrusively on a clump of sumac berries; from the pokiest turtle inching his way across a back country road of Pictured Rocks to the fleetest bobcat stalking an unwary prey; from the gentlest butterfly sipping nectar in a field of thistles to the deadliest rattlesnake sunning on a fallen log in the forgotten marsh he knows as home.

Although some species of game birds and mammals may be hunted within the confines of National Wildlife Refuges such as the 95,000 acre Seney National Wildlife Refuge in the Upper Peninsula, these wetlands greatly abet the survival of Michigan's rich and varied fauna associated with water and its adjacent habitats. With the aid of this nationwide system, the Canada goose has staged a remarkable comeback in many locales, and his form now adorns all signs marking our National Wildlife Refuges. We can only hope that the same success will occur with other transient waterfowl visitors to Michigan such as the threatened canvasback, a strikingly-marked duck highly prized by hunters for his sumptuous taste.

Conservationists trust that another such beneficiary will be the fish-eating bald eagle. Unquestionably the most impressive bird in our state, this magnificent raptor soars on wings that span seven feet before entering a power dive exceeding 100 miles per hour. Although the bald eagle still successfully nests in Michigan, he sorely needs the help of the people who chose him their symbol if he is to remain our national emblem. In addition to eagles, at Seney you may still tune in the clattering call of migrating sandhill cranes, a memorable sound which thrills amateur and veteran birdwatchers alike. You might even hear the hollow cry of the attractively marked loon as his ghostly wail splits the morning silence of fog-banked lakes.

At Shiawassee National Wildlife Refuge, you can gaze upon thousands of geese and whistling swans, stopping over on their way to wintering grounds further south. At Wyandotte National Wildlife Refuge, located in the Detroit River only ten miles south of the car capital of the world, thousands of diving ducks congregate to feed upon the plentiful stands of wild celery. In all, more than 300 species of birds visit or nest in Michigan, adding color, diversity and beauty to our state.

Michigan maintains 80 state parks that offer an almost infinite variety of recreational contacts with the outdoors that may range from a Sunday afternoon of tossing frisbees at Dodge Brothers State Park Number Four just outside Detroit to a week of wilderness backpacking across the 58,000 acre Porcupine Mountains State Park at the western tip of the Upper Peninsula, some 600 highway miles distant.

Beyond its woods and waters, Michigan exhibits an admirable diversity of other natural landscapes. There are miles of sand dunes and beaches stretching out along Lake Michigan and Lake Huron. There is the mineral-stained, rocky coastline of Lake Superior. A good deal of hilly terrain may be enjoyed in the southeast and, though we have no deserts, you still may come upon prickly pear cactus blooming in the sandy regions near Newaygo. We also have mountains and, although they are not the cloud-piercing peaks of the west, the Porcupine and the Huron Mountains in the rugged northwestern segment of the Upper Peninsula attain Michigan's highest altitudes in the neighborhood of 2,000 feet and form some of the highest elevations in the mid-west.

There are peninsulas such as Keweenaw and Old Mission whose slender fingers of land dare to probe farther into the waters than the remainder of the timid mainland hand. There are islands enough to satisfy any vacationer, including treasure troves such as historic Beaver Island lying about 30 miles offshore in northern Lake Michigan. Here, in 1847, James Jesse Strang organized a Mormon colony and three years later crowned himself king, thereby establishing this land as the site of the only "Kingdom" ever to exist in America.

Man's influence upon the landscape has further altered the face of the state by introducing landforms with the military precision of such features as the vineyards in the southwest. Other agricultural contours were created by farmlands that bear apples and cherries, strawberries and peaches, corn and celery, field beans and tomatoes, beets and potatoes. Combined with a not-to-be-overlooked production of cattle, sheep and pigs, this fertile agriculture gives Michigan its diversified rural character and produces a revenue for the state that, until 1976, was traditionally second only to manufacturing.

So it is with Michigan. This land so rich in geologic history, natural grandeur and human lore from the past, is yet today a wonderland of natural splendor, agricultural abundance and human interest.

Evergreen and birch grove along shore of small inland lake, in Ludington State Park.

Young tamarack cones, less than one inch long, mature to chestnut brown. This tree, commonly called larch, will shed its needles each autumn. Right: Tahquamenon Falls, near Newberry. Upper and Lower Falls in the Tahquamenon River referred to in Longfellow's Hiawatha. Pages 28 and 29 following: Fishermen enjoy a period of pleasure in Lake Michigan.

Evidence of Canada goose directed toward nearby woods reveals his yen for wandering. Left: Grass anchors the surface of Grand Sable Dunes, subject to the steady winds off Lake Superior.

Pine needles layered with light dusting of frost reflect the chill of winter. Right: Mid-winter wind blows through forest southwest of Whitefish Bay in the upper Peninsula.

Lights delineate the
Mackinac Bridge at dusk.
It is among the longest and
most beautiful suspension
bridges in the world. Left:
Sun highlights the capitol
dome at Lansing, dedi-
cated in 1879. It was
named the state capital
in 1847.

Red fox on the alert for rodents in northern region of state. They are among the smartest of our wild animals, found in many areas across the U.S.A. Right: The state's trees, referred to as "green gold" in the heyday of logging, annually burst into natural gold each fall.

Frosty coating on choke cherry leaf defines seasonal change. Left: Rows of field beans stretch for distant horizon, protected by windbreak of mixed conifers and hardwoods. Agriculture is dominant factor in this region adjacent to Big Bay de Noc. Pages 40 and 41 following: Gale force winds give birth to spectacular cloud formations over Lake Superior.

Birthplace of Luther Burbank, moved from Lancaster, Massachusetts to become part of collection in Greenfield Village and the Henry Ford Museum. He was an early horticulturist responsible for many important achievements in growth of peanuts and potatoes. Right: Tulips all aglow in May, signal arrival of festival time in Holland. Settled by the Dutch in 1847, it is the tulip center of our country. Pages 44 and 45 following: Morning sun accentuates surface vapor on Wildwing Lake in early spring.

Ice on Huron River at
Delhi Rapids is chilling
reminder of the winter of
1977. Left: The last traces
of winter linger in William
Holliday Park, west of
Detroit; an area to be
enjoyed in its natural
beauty and preserved
intact for future genera-
tions. It is truly irreplaceable.

Teeming color in a truck-load of peaches is exceeded only by the astonishing abundance of the state's annual harvest of fruit. Left: Morning sun creates a glow atop mixed oak trees on Goose Island in Wildwing Lake, Kensington Metropark.

The clear water of Lake Huron bares the rocky shoreline north of Alpena. Right: Laughing Whitefish Falls tumbles through a forest corridor southwest of Munising. Pages 56 and 57 following: Spectacular panorama west of Negaunee in the Upper Peninsula.

The Big Spring, Kitch-iti-kipi, meaning Mirror of the Heavens, pours forth 16,000 gallons of water per minute northwest of Manistique. Left: The gorgeous Calypso orchid, a threatened species, displays its delicate form in the piny woods of Wilderness State Park, on Lake Michigan. Pages 60 and 61 following: Morning shadows across a blanket of snow in Tahquamenon State Park.

Pine trees along the rim of Black River Gorge north of Ironwood near the Wisconsin border. Right: Mullein, the common name of genus of woolly herbs belonging to the figwort family. It can be found in areas of the state where it is not too damp.

The skyline of downtown
Detroit as it appears from
Belle Isle, looking across
the Detroit River. Left:
Redwood crucifix
dominates shrine in Indian
River, approximately 30
miles south of Mackinac
Bridge. It supports a seven
ton statue of Christ on a
55 foot cross, weighing
14 tons; carved from
single redwood log.

Birthplace of Henry Ford, moved to Greenfield Village and the Henry Ford Museum in 1944. He was born in Dearborn 1863 and organized the Ford Motor Company in 1903. Right: Agate Falls, on middle fork of the Ontonagon River, near Trout Creek.

The Fallasburg Bridge, erected in the 1860's, spans the Flat River near Lowell. It is one of only six covered bridges remaining in the state. Left: Birch foliage in early fall reflected on the calm water of the Manistique River. More than 36,000 miles of streams and rivers crisscross the state.

The rugged coastline of
Keweenaw Peninsula at
Copper Harbor. This
northernmost tip of the
state was once called its
Treasure Chest. Right:
From this aerial perch a
bald eagle, proud symbol
of our land, surveys the
kingdom over which he is
the unchallenged master.
Pages 72 and 73 following:
Icy morning in low-
lands of Seney National
Wildlife Refuge, northeast
of Manistique.

Delicate body structure of an elongated crane-fly resting on wild strawberry plant. Left: High winds drive the waters of Lake Superior into the rocky shoreline of Keweenaw Peninsula. Pages 76 and 77 following: Nature's handiwork fully exposed in Isle Royale National Park.

Eyes of this green amphibian prove that he is looking in your direction. Right: Dense growth of white pine in Hartwick Pines State Park north of Camp Grayling. It is the last stand of virgin white pine remaining in the state.

Ice landscape on Lake Michigan east of Manistique is reminiscent of the lunar surface. Left: Porcupine appears relaxed in northern woods. Well protected against predators, armed with approximately 20,000 quills, they are frequently quite conspicuous.

Vapor hovers over surface
of the Tahquamenon River
as it heads toward the
Lower Falls. Right: Thin
veil of clouds diffuse the
light of the sun creating a
rare mid-winter scene.

The traditional weather-worn barn exhibits many individual variations of the time-honored theme which still dots many acres of the rural landscape. Left: Munising Falls thinly conceals layered limestone formation in Pictured Rocks National Lakeshore.

Swamp grass chilled by the frigid temperature of mid-winter lies dormant, creating a maze of whites and browns. Right: Siberian tiger reigns supreme in the Detroit Zoo. The staff has gained an international reputation for its efforts on behalf of this endangered species. Pages 88 and 89 following: Sand dunes are dominant feature of state park near Ludington.

Striking colors of this Ctenucha moth make him one of our most attractive insects. Left: Law quad, University of Michigan, Ann Arbor. Founded at Detroit in 1817 it was moved to present location in 1837. Pages 92 and 93 following: Rugged shoreline of Lake Superior in Copper Country.

Popular Gorge Falls readily accessible along Black River Drive outside Ironwood and Bessemer. Right: Spiked shadows of an abandoned fortress indicative of protection offered restored cabin of old Fort Wilkins. It was established to shelter miners in the Keweenaw district from threat of local Indians.

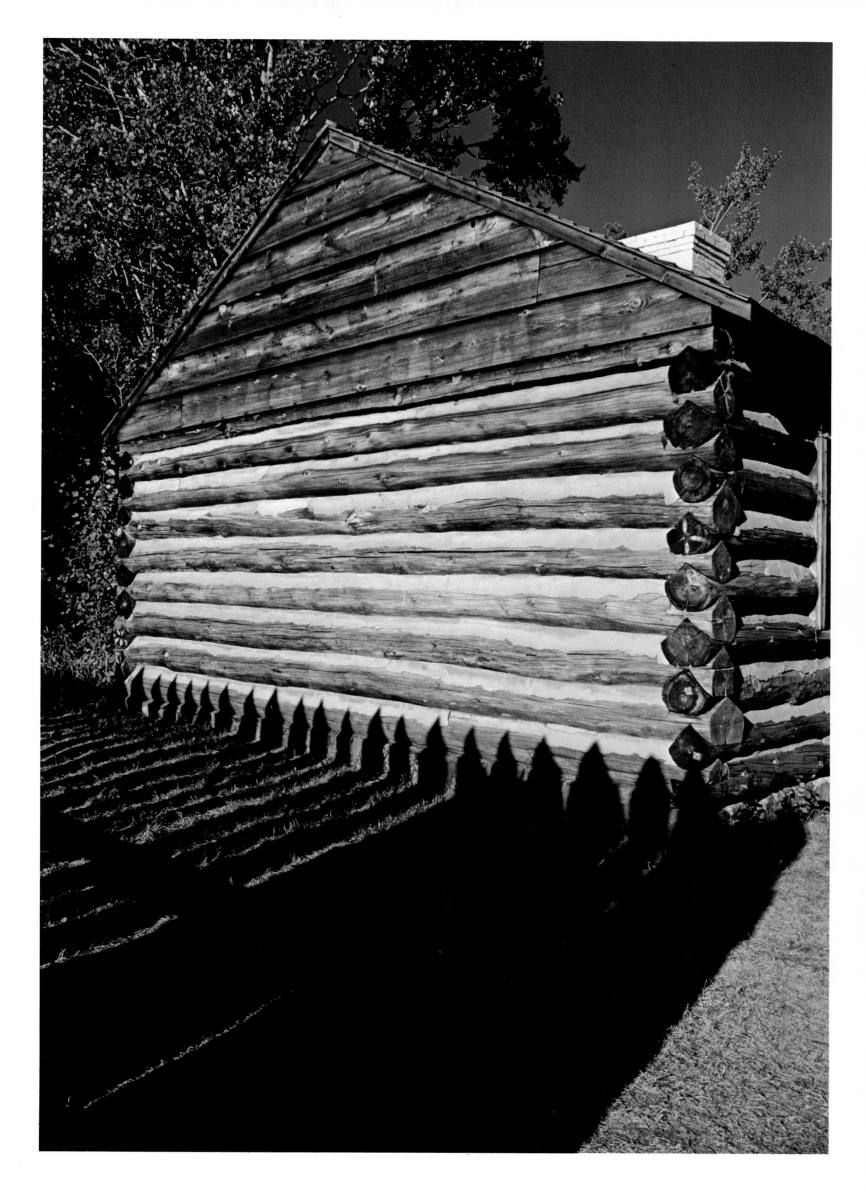

The many forms of sycamore bark provide a never ending study. Left: Irregular texture of fallen snow contrasts with rushing water to symbolically show many faces of winter above shore of Lake Superior.

Unique detail of cedar limb in late afternoon sunlight on Isle Royale National Park. Right: Gentle flow of east branch of Fox River is clearly defined along snow covered banks.

Fallen tree adorned with heavy frost reveals the delicate lacework of nature in Kensington Metropark. Left: Horse Race Rapids on the Paint River in the Upper Peninsula tumble over mighty boulders on river bed.

Falls of the Presque Isle
River cascade through
Porcupine Mountains
State Park to eventually
enter Lake Superior. Right:
Fall foliage stresses the
eternal beauty of white
birch in Ottawa National
Forest. Pages 104 and 105
following: View looking
north from the Cut River
Bridge in the direction
of Lake Superior.

A mixed hemlock/hard-
wood forest clearly defines
Lake of the Clouds,
famous landmark in
Porcupine Mountains
State Park. Right: Canada
goose welcomes the
arrival of spring to again
enjoy a diet of tasty duck-
weed. Pages 108 and 109
following: One of many
exposures composing
Kensington Metropark.

Massive column of ice
fronts Tahquamenon Falls
between Newberry and
Paradise. Right: Pictured
Rocks National Lakeshore
along the shore of Lake
Superior. View looking
east from Miner's Beach.

Frost covered cattails create a delicate pattern when viewed at close range. Left: The Huron River at Delhi Rapids outside Ann Arbor.

Highbush-cranberries savored by grouse and pheasant offer brilliant display of color in early September. Right: Taking advantage of the state's superb water recreation, sailboats speckle the water of many lakes.

Freezing winter temperatures deactivate Gorge Falls on the Black River near the Wisconsin border. Left: Dense fog tempered the rays of mid-morning sun over icy pond luring area geese.

White birch yields striking contrast with the brilliant blue sky along the Au Sable River, north of Tawas City. Right: The Black River just prior to its entry into mighty Lake Superior. Pages 120 and 121 following: Yellow goldenrod and pink fireweed turned to seed signal the coming of autumn along Cliff Drive in the Upper Peninsula.

Camera captured unusual shaft of light entering forest canopy to highlight stream in William Holliday Park, west of Detroit. Left: View from under side of Tahquamenon. This camera position proved to be extremely hazardous. Pages 124 and 125 following: Lone rock void of ice appears misplaced along the edge of Lake Michigan near Manistique.

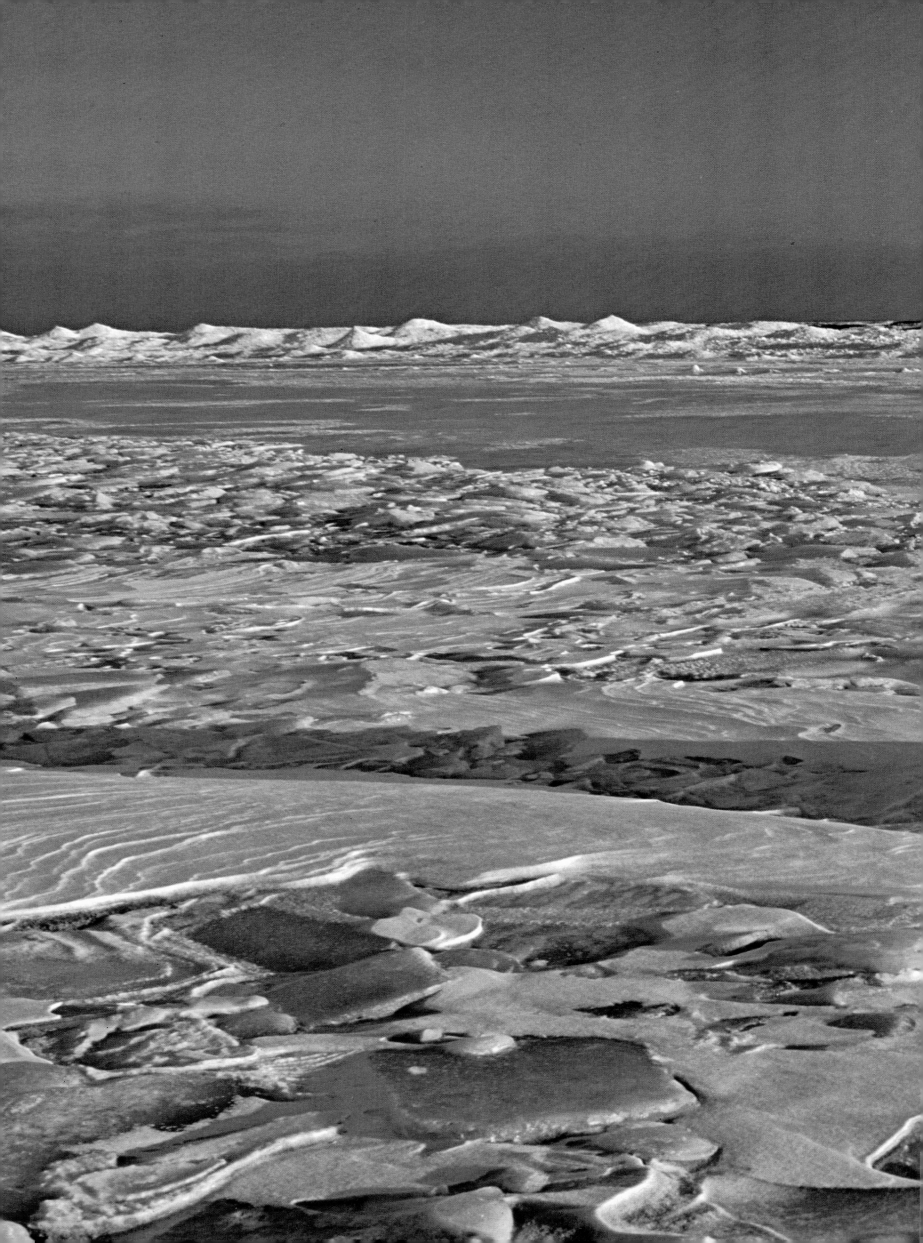

Sundew plants supplement their diet by capturing insects in beads of sticky fluid at ends of projecting hairs. Right: Sun and mist combine to envelop moisture laden area on a cool spring morning.